SILENT LANGUAGE
IN THE CLASSROOM

By Charles Galloway

Library of Congress Catalog Card Number: 76-23912
ISBN 0-87367-086-8
Copyright © 1976 by The Phi Delta Kappa Educational Foundation
Bloomington, Indiana

TABLE OF CONTENTS

TABLE OF CONTENTS

UNDERSTANDING OUR SILENT LANGUAGE

Although several minutes had passed since Mr. Sampson gave the seatwork assignment, Jim was looking out the window, unaware of the other students and the passing time.

Suddenly Jim realized that Mr. Sampson was looking directly at him. He sensed that the teacher was ready to tell him to get busy. What should he do? He cared about what Mr. Sampson thought of him. He did not want to be embarrassed; he had not meant to appear uninterested in the assignment.

Wanting to let Mr. Sampson know his feelings, Jim began to feign concentrated thought. He looked up and then down at his paper, frowning as if mentally groping with one of the assigned problems. He hoped that Mr. Sampson would accept his efforts to redefine the situation, to correct his mistake.

From habit acquired in teaching, Mr. Sampson felt compelled to reenforce what his gaze had said without words and sharply remarked, "All right, Jim, let's get to work. You don't have much time to finish this assignment."

Because Jim believed that Mr. Sampson knew he was trying to show his willingness to work, he heard more than the teacher's words. He also heard, "Don't ask me to ignore your daydreaming. You have made a mistake and I'm here to remind you." For Jim, the reminders are further proof of his worst fears—that he is no good, that he can't do anything right.

If you had observed this incident, what would be your impression? Simply a minor misunderstanding that occurs in the classroom all the time? This youngster will not daydream again when there is work to be done because the teacher didn't let him get away with it? Or do you believe that Mr. Sampson should learn that silence is sometimes the best communication, that he should pay more attention to his behavior patterns and those of his students?

Your impression of the incident may reveal how aware you now are of the impact of nonverbal communication in the classroom. You may realize that the communication between the teacher and the student had little to do with the words spoken. Both were interpreting the actions and the behaviors of the other. Both knew that the facial expressions, the gestures, the actions, and the nonverbal behaviors of others speak as loudly as words. Both have learned in dealing with other people that what is not said may be more meaningful than what is said.

Nonverbal communication is present in every face-to-face conversation. A person instinctively watches those he talks with to determine whether they are interested in and understand the spoken words. Routinely he glances into the other person's face at the end of a statement. While talking, he notices the other person's posture, body movements, and gestures as additional indicators of interest and understanding. The listener is "hearing" not only the words chosen by the speaker but also the inflections in his voice, the movement of his eyes, and his stance. If their exchange goes well, a rhythmic balance of give and take occurs.

When I began, more than fifteen years ago, to study the value of nonverbal communication for education, only researchers considered it a field of serious study and a potentially practical tool for improving communications and relationships. This was true though nonverbal communication preceded verbal communication. We can be sure that early people relied on gestures, facial expressions, and eye contact to judge companions and enemies before developing a system of verbal languages.

In our modern society, actors, dancers, lawyers, sales representatives, diplomats, and writers have always been aware of the impact of gesture, voice inflection, and body posture on their messages. The most successful of these professionals have learned both to read others' body language and to manage and control their own for a desired effect.

A number of popular books on the subject of nonverbal communication have made more people in every walk of life aware of its existence. Those who believe it may be no more than a fad have not realized that nonverbal messages are the persistent companions of every word we speak. Perhaps too much emphasis has been given to reading signs and signals, simple gestures, and facial expressions for clues to another's feelings. If a person clenches his teeth, he's angry; if he looks down or avoids eye contact, he's embarrassed or fearful; if he opens his arms, he is receptive or can be trusted. Such interpretations of gestures and expressions as easy-to-read indicators of emotions have been overplayed.

Communication, both verbal and nonverbal, is complex. Few nonverbal gestures, perhaps none, precisely reflect internal feelings. Indeed, it can be dangerous and presumptuous to assume that a few expressions will reveal another person's true beliefs or feelings. No dictionary of gestures is available. Each of us writes our interpretations of nonverbal behaviors during human contacts without assurance that our working dictionary is valid and reliable.

During our lifetime, each of us has been exposed to thousands of nonverbal expressions and signs. We know what a face can express, what a gesture can imply, and what a movement denotes because our experiences in countless contacts with other persons have taught us. We count on these multiple signs and signals, these examples of nonverbal language, to let us know where we stand and to signify what is real.

If you doubt your knowledge and understanding of nonverbal information, ask yourself this: How many facial expressions have you seen? What have you done with all those impressions? Nothing? That is unlikely. Most of us have stored those impressions into mind sets. Based on this working vocabulary of facial expressions, we are able to read a face as clearly as a word on a printed page. If it is a familiar word, we know its meaning. And the same can be said for a facial expression. Just as we might be unsure about a word's definition, a facial expression can confuse us. Words or facial expressions will be missed in a conversation. But once in a while a word has special significance, and so does a facial expression. A look of surprise, elation, or anger can be spotted in a millisecond and makes a difference.

What is Nonverbal Communication?

Whenever human beings come into contact, a reality is understood and shared without words. This fundamental assumption undergirds the significance of nonverbal communication. More occurs between people than an exchange of words. Nonverbal communication consists not only of facial expressions and body gestures but also of the way a person uses space and time. Nonverbal behaviors are the primary vehicles for expressing emotion. Behaviors, better than words, convey hate, fear, anger, and anxiety. What is difficult to put into words often finds its way through facial expression, gesture, and movement.

The messages conveyed by behavior cannot be interpreted outside their context. A still photograph of a grimacing face can tell us that the person is experiencing or pretending an emotion, but unless we know the situation in which the grimace occurred, it cannot be interpreted to add to our understanding of another person.

Nonverbal behavior can be described as a relationship language. Silent cues signal a change or provide continuity to interpersonal relationships. These cues, whether by face, eyes, or gesture, can be the primary means of expressing intimacy, aloofness, concern, or indifference.

Nonverbal behaviors are qualifiers that indicate how verbal statements ought to be understood. Behavioral scientists and psychiatrists have described nonverbal behavior as a "leakage channel" that is difficult to control or to censor. Simply put, nonverbal behavior is more likely to reveal true emotions and feelings and is less likely to be deceptive than verbal communication. Nonverbal behaviors give away how we feel about what we say.

We are free to choose the words we use, but we do not have as much control over our behaviors. We can hear our words as we speak them and correct wrong choices, but we cannot see ourselves as others see us. Many people are unaware of the impression their body language conveys to others.

Successful courtroom lawyers, diplomats, and used car salesmen are often cited as people who have learned to manage the impressions they give to others. Despite the successes of some, nonverbal cues are generally less manageable and more revealing than verbal information. Some of our personal nonverbal language is learned as part of our role in our culture. Indeed, researchers say that our culture has as much influence on our nonverbal language as it has on verbal language.

Anthropologists, sociologists, psychologists, and educators are currently bringing new insights to the emerging field of nonverbal behaviors. Anthropologists are looking for cultural differences and similarities in body language. They are especially interested in how nonverbal languages are learned and the unique forms the behaviors take in cultural expression. Sociologists are exploring the nonverbal behaviors associated with different roles and occupations. They talk about strategic interactions, discrepant roles, and territorial regions. As might be expected, psychologists are looking for the connections between nonverbal behaviors and personality and motivation. Educators are examining the nonverbal aspects of teaching and learning. Traditionally, teaching has been considered a predominantly verbal skill. Teachers talk, students listen and recite. Research has already shown that how well a teacher teaches also depends on the nonverbal communication carried on with the students, both individually and collectively.

With nonverbal behavior defined and researched, do we have data that we can trust to improve communications between people? Are there guidelines for interpreting nonverbal behaviors that can be used by the average person to heighten understanding of others and self? Just becoming conscious of nonverbal behaviors can provide added information and insight to the person who is sensitive to this way of communicating. But we must remember that nonverbal information stands alongside verbal influences. The sources of message sending and receiving provide the total message.

Why should we be concerned with nonverbal communication at all? What difference does it make? The answer I like best is to better understand ourselves and others. The key to uncovering the value of the nonverbal is to recognize its relationship to what we are and to what we communicate. There is no truth like the whole truth. Nonverbal expressions provide a fuller measure of what we want to communicate.

NONVERBAL COMMUNICATION IN THE CLASSROOM

Teacher behaviors have always been recognized as classroom management skills. You may remember, as a beginning teacher, being warned, "Don't let the kids see you smile before Christmas." Any physical sign of warmth and friendliness, any lapse from a stern, no-nonsense demeanor would inevitably lead to unruly classes.

Now educators are beginning to understand the greater significance of nonverbal behaviors in the classroom as an instructional tool and as a trademark of student-teacher relationships. That nonverbal communication has only recently been seen as a positive tool of teaching is no surprise. Much of instruction is based on verbal skills, on talking, on writing, on listening, on using words to express and receive information. The first-grader who was asked by his father to define teaching said, after less than a minute's reflection, "Dad, teaching is talking."

Certainly when a teacher teaches, he talks. Direct observations of classrooms are the basis for the "rule of two-thirds." Two-thirds of the time in the classroom someone is talking. Usually, it is the teacher who is lecturing, giving directions, or criticizing behavior.

Teachers tell students much more than they express with words. Their facial expressions, gestures, postures, vocal pauses, position in the classroom, movement or lack of movement, and dozens of other behaviors express messages that are usually accurately received by the students.

Teachers learn to use their eyes to convey messages to students. They stare; they look over the tops of their glasses; they wink; they narrow their eyes. A certain glance says clearly, "Stop that!" Another look says, "Will I need to speak to you?" Anyone who visits classrooms can see that students understand these eye messages, these silent instructions, urgings, and admonitions.

Teachers are not the only ones using nonverbal behaviors to convey and receive messages in the classroom. The students read each gesture and glance of their teachers. Even the very youngest student will not show any doubt when asked, "Who is your teacher's pet? Is she afraid of the principal? Does she like boys more than girls?" Children know these answers because they read attitudes by observing nonverbal cues.

Ask a second-grader to repeat the teacher's words used to scold a classmate and you will get a blank look or faltering attempts. But ask seven-year-old Jane to show you how the teacher looked when she was scolding Terry, and you will see the postures and poses of a scolding teacher, replete with gestures and expressions.

Because nonverbal communication is so much a part of what is happening in the classroom, it should be and is assuming a greater importance in the training of teachers and others in education. In school, it is the teacher's communication that makes the difference, for the student is rarely insulated from the teacher. The student is in a position to be the most seriously victimized by difficulties in communication. Just as the teacher's spoken words should be appropriate to the child's experiences and consistent with the teacher's meanings, so too should non-verbal messages be appropriate and consistent.

In their nonverbal behavior, teachers tell individual students a lot about how they feel about the students as persons. Through behavior teachers can express information that they would never have the courage or cruelty to state verbally and would retract if they knew the student had decoded the information.

Nonverbal Communication and Involvement

Important as it is in the classroom, nonverbal communication is not restricted to students and teacher. It is just as much a factor in corridors, committee meetings, evaluation sessions, and parent-teacher conferences.

Anywhere in the school setting that two or more people are working on a task, one of them will surely say, "The problem is communication." Communication is difficult and complex. Poor communication, symptomatic of the inability or unwillingness of people to relate to one another, is frequently the stumbling block to achieving goals, but part of the problem may be that we are not aware of what we are communicating. Through our nonverbal language we may be leaking messages and communicating much more than we know.

All of us, students, teachers, parents, want to be where we are recognized and appreciated. All of us watch for the glance, the greeting, the nonverbal cue which says, "I see you, I know you are there." If we also receive verbal and nonverbal cues that indicate "I'm glad you are here, I cherish your existence, you have value," then we are likely to take the risk of participation and interaction. We are willing to try to communicate.

We feel free to participate when we feel included. The initial contact that indicates acknowledgement and value makes us willing to enter into the communication. More often than not, we are reading nonverbal behaviors when we receive these feelings of inclusion. Conversely, feelings of exclusion ultimately breed detachment and alienation, and we receive these feelings from reading others' nonverbal behavior. Only rarely does anyone in a public institution such as a school tell others verbally that they are excluded from participation, though often nonverbal behavior will tell them just that.

Just as a pattern of nonverbal messages of exclusion can eventually lead the student to feelings of alienation from the school, so the same pattern imposed on teachers, custodians, secretaries, aides, and parents can lead to a feeling that no one cares. When we believe that no one cares, we protect our self-esteem by acting as though we do not care about the institution or the people in it. In large schools, it is not impossible for a teacher to drive into the parking lot, enter the building, begin a teaching day, spend time in the lounge, and return home without receiving any indication from another adult in the building that his presence made any difference that day.

A frequent complaint of educators is how can we get students, parents, and other citizens to participate in solving educational problems? Involvement does not come easy; it requires a trusting environment and a psychologically safe haven for effort. Individuals are free to become involved only when they do not need to use their energies to claim their existence or to prove their value. When we express needs for a better sense of community in the school, or better staff relations, or individualized instruction in the classroom without committing ourselves to communicative contact that includes both verbal and nonverbal messages, we expect the impossible.

Humaneness and the Study of Communication

No matter what his philosophy of education, the student of nonverbal communication will be inescapably drawn to the humanistic approach. After examining the variables that influence nonverbal understanding, he will see the frailty of the human condition and the powerlessness of many persons to be understood well, if at all. He begins to see that many nonverbal messages, including some cloaked in inappropriate behaviors, are the cries and calls of fellow human beings who cannot make an unperceptive and insensitive world aware that they need to be recognized and to be given a chance to live an existence with meaning.

Nonverbal communication and humanistic values become partners because the nonverbal provides sources of information not available in verbal communication. It can be assumed that the more information a person possesses about himself and others, the more humanely he will behave. We know that with limited knowledge or incorrect information people infer inaccurate estimates of other people and events. A lack of information tends to confirm one's fears and is often the reason for inhumanity. Of course, a humanistic response to others' needs never guarantees humanism, nor does it insure good behaviors from students, but the approach makes it difficult for the other person to act badly.

For educators, for all those concerned with fostering the growth of others and establishing dependable channels of communication, these questions rest at the heart of the study of nonverbal communication:

- Am I aware of my nonverbal messages to students? to my colleagues? to parents?

15

- Am I willing to take a responsibility for my nonverbal influences on others?
- Am I aware of the nonverbal messages of others?
- Am I willing to be influenced and to care about others' nonverbal messages?

Nonverbal Communication in Humanistic Management

Slamming the car door, Ms. Franklin, the principal, began her customary brisk walk to the front door of the building. A few students were standing near the entrance but she didn't see them. She was in a hurry. The students noticed her but were not surprised that she did not say "good morning."

Ms. Franklin did greet her secretary but did not look at her as she walked to her office door. She closed the door and began her day.

Unless there was an emergency, no one would enter the office without being summoned. The secretary would handle teachers and students by referring them to the assistant principal or the guidance counselor. Ms. Franklin would be busy with paperwork and her correspondence with the central office.

What can be inferred from this account? Nothing, until we realize that this pattern is repeated every day. This is a principal who rarely speaks to teachers except in formal meetings, who never speaks to students unless they have a serious problem, and who would rather work with statistics than with people.

When people are admitted to her office, Ms. Franklin sits behind the desk and rarely looks at them when they talk. She can use direct eye contact, however, when her authority is required. Ms. Franklin likes being an administrator but becomes irritated with bothersome teacher-student conflicts that demand her attention.

Being appointed to an administrative position does not necessarily mean that a person has had a successful history of contacts with others. Nevertheless, the most frequently witnessed behaviors in any organization are speaking and listening. We have to talk to each other, and we need to listen. If we are to accomplish the goals of an organization, particularly those of a school, we must be able to give information to others as well as receive it.

It is difficult to understand how an administrator can expect to receive meaningful information from the staff without inviting their communication. The nonverbal behaviors that encourage or inhibit communication in the classroom operate in the school office as well.

If the principal invites the teacher to the office for a conference, we might expect that her nonverbal behavior would encourage communication. But this is not always so. If she sits behind the desk, frequently checks her watch, and does not look at the teacher who is talking, she may not learn much of value in the conference. Although the verbal invitation to talk about a new project or a problem may seem genuine, her nonverbal behavior is not congruent. Remembering that it is a human tendency to rely more on the nonverbal than the verbal when messages seem mixed, we will not be surprised if the conference produces little real communication.

The day-by-day contacts within an organization make us feel better or worse about ourselves. Few of us are the self-actualizing persons described by Abraham Maslow. We are not secure enough about our own abilities to risk participation unless we are openly invited to do so. We need to feel that we are doing our jobs well and that others understand us, but we must have verbal and nonverbal indicators to prove this.

The climate of our organization will tell us something about ourselves. If it is a warm, open climate, we will be able to take risks, to try the new, to offer our most original thoughts, and to act creatively. If it is a repressive climate, we will not make any move that threatens our job security and our self-image.

The single most important factor in determining the climate of an organization is the top executive. If the superintendent supports and encourages the participation and involvement of principals, they in turn will encourage the participation of teachers and students in making the school a better place to be.

During the past several years I have worked with educators at every level. Generalizing from these contacts, I have found that administrators are capable observers of behavior. They seem to have developed an awareness of behavioral meanings and significance. I have heard them say again and again: "I notice how a person shakes hands, stands, walks, listens, and smiles. I look at his general appearance, his hairstyle, and his attitude."

But here is the paradox. I have found that while administrators are busily looking and analyzing, they fail to understand what their own behaviors mean to others. They are surprised to learn that others make the same observations about them. This may be an occupational hazard of being an administrator. Believing that they have the upper hand, they overestimate their power and authority and underestimate the way others may react.

Several administrators have told me that they are careful not to communicate nonverbally. They have argued that sitting still, assuming a stoic expression, and maintaining a distance from their staff will prevent any misreading of their intentions or wishes. This is, of course, a naive view of human contact. There is no escape from communicating, and there is no such thing as nonbehavior. We are always behaving, and others are always reading our behavior. Both a successful administrator and a successful teacher behave congruently with their words, and both their verbal and nonverbal behavior invites the participation of all involved in the education processes.

HOW THE UNSPOKEN, UNWRITTEN CURRICULUM OPERATES

To better understand the dimensions of nonverbal communication in the school setting, let us examine how the school joins with the family and friends to teach all students the rudiments of nonverbal language.

Within the first few days of school, a five-year-old begins to learn a network of nonverbal signals and signs that are connected to the rules and regulations of the school. Talking, sitting, standing, walking, and playing are done on schedule and command. It's no easy task for the child to master these matters of deportment and ritualized acts of behavior. It becomes particularly difficult because the child's top priority at the time is to gain the attention and approval of a new adult.

Sometimes a behavior displeases the teacher. The child, eager to earn approval and prove to himself that he is smart and able to "go to school," begins to rely on the teacher's responses to learn how to look and act like a student, much as he depended on his parents' reactions earlier to learn how to act like a good boy. He doesn't know exactly what a good boy or a good student is, but he knows adults' reactions to his acts. Unfortunately, few adults assist children in learning acceptable behavior. They simply point out misbehaviors and errors, leaving the rest of the definition to the child.

In playing the new student role, the child soon discovers the significance of hand raising, which is not learned at home. In school, the raised hand is the way to "get your turn," to be recognized. When one student answers a question, others learn to

19

lower their hands. The teacher does not reward repeated answers. When the teacher asks a question, the primary students' hands fly up in all directions. The very young believe that a display of enthusiasm makes a difference. However, some teachers disdain waving hands, and the perceptive child quickly learns this. Some students wave their hands to be chosen and hold their arms to show their patience.

Later on, the student will learn to raise his hand so he will *not* be called on. Third- and fourth-graders learn this nonverbal message well because their teachers are the first to put them in a position where they may have to falsify their behavior. The teacher asks, "How many of you read your homework assignment?" Not to raise one's hand is to lose self-esteem by publicly testifying to one's irresponsibility. Believing perhaps that the students have read their assignment, the teacher begins by asking a simple question. Even though the student doesn't want to be called on, he raises his hand again. If he doesn't raise his hand for an easy question, the teacher will know that he did not read the assignment.

By this time, the student has learned to add other nonverbal signs and signals to avoid being chosen. He raises his hand but neither waves it nor holds it aloft timidly. He looks at the teacher, but not in her eyes. He doesn't look out the window or down at the floor, for either of these will draw her attention. If the teacher does call on him, he will stutter and stall because teachers don't wait for answers—they call on another student. Or he will pretend that he didn't intend to have his hand up; it was just habit. Whether the hand-raising ploy works or not, it is something that must be done to protect the student's self-image.

Throughout his school years, the student will be developing and refining a repertoire of nonverbal language, usually for the same reason—to maintain standing in the teacher's eyes. Pretending to listen in class, appearing busy during seatwork assignments, and seeming interested in the uninteresting are games that children learn to play with no verbal instructions about the rules.

Matter of Survival

All the time the student is learning to send nonverbal messages, he is learning to read the adult's nonverbal messages. By interpreting and inferring from nonverbal cues, students seek a fuller understanding of the teacher. When the nonverbal cues are not congruent with the verbal, they accept the nonverbal as the more valid.

If the student came into contact with a teacher only a few times and not daily, nonverbal cues might not be so significant in teaching and learning. But the student must depend on interpreting the teacher's nonverbal behavior to sustain his own image. The forces of power, control, influence, motivation, self-esteem, and interpersonal relationships are all related to the interplays of nonverbal exchanges. In fact, a student who misinterprets the teacher's behavior becomes confused and uncertain.

It is well known that teachers invite discipline problems when their behavior is inconsistent with their verbal messages.

> His first day in class, the new student along with others settled down to work when the teacher warned that he would "brook no nonsense." Later in the morning, the students began to talk and move around, and the teacher seemed undisturbed. At noon, one of the students explained to the new boy, "Well, when he said to keep quiet and work, he really meant it. But we've kinda learned his ways. It's the way he sits or looks or something. . . . Anyway, we knew when he didn't really mean it anymore."

Silent signals let students know what their teachers think about them. Almost every time a teacher talks with a student, he shares his evaluation of the young person. By the way he speaks to a student, by the amount of time he devotes to him, and by the number of times he chooses to approach the student, the teacher conveys, without using a single word of praise or criticism, his impression that the student is smart, slow, important, or unimportant. Even when the teacher routinely says, "Get busy," he may give a look that the student can only interpret as, "He thinks I'm lazy."

Because nonverbal communication is especially critical in the teacher-student relationship, it should be used in positive ways to involve and include the student in learning processes. Learning to give as much attention to nonverbal cues employed in instruction as we give to the verbal ones can open a rich new source of information about our students.

Using Nonverbal Behaviors as Instructional Tools

As teachers, we do many things that are not in our students' best interests and not in our best interests. We give much support and encouragement verbally and nonverbally to the student who needs it least and little to the student who needs it most. These mistakes cannot be avoided entirely, but they can be prevented from occurring each day of the school year.

One of the purposes of school is to help students and others grow in self-confidence and self-esteem. One way to encourage self-esteem in others and in ourselves is to provide *focused attention.* This means taking time to share yourself and providing time for the student to share himself.

Most teachers highly value physical and emotional distance. It is the nonverbal behavior that says, "I am the teacher and you are the students. Don't forget it." Distance does not encourage communication. Most relationships between teacher and students are not close, and, as a result, teachers do not communicate well with students.

Teachers are quick to point out that they do not have time to become close to many of the students they see each day. No one can argue with that. But it can be argued that a teacher can try to have a close relationship with more than one student and can involve at least one student who feels excluded and needs to feel included. Teachers can also become more aware of the nonverbal instructing that accompanies the verbal. They can reexamine their movements in the classroom and the gestures that have been acquired in their occupational role.

Physical proximity intensifies other body messages. If a teacher approaches or stands close to a student, scolding seems more severe and the compliment more genuine and worthwhile.

Standing with arms folded across the chest psychologically removes the teacher from the class activity. It effectively lets the class know that the teacher will return when certain prerequisites—silence, cleared desk tops, student attention—are met.

Touching, the most powerful nonverbal signal, can be the most dangerous or the most pleasurable. In our society, strangers do not touch. If they do accidently, the offending person is quick to apologize. But a loving touch is a powerful tool at the teacher's disposal. Recent surveys showed that 90 percent of children aged 7 to 10 welcomed hugging and patting from both parents and

22

teachers. Older students, more aware of society's taboos, preferred arm squeezes, pats on the back, and quick, one-armed shoulder hugs.

While eye *contact* is frequently employed to manage and discipline classes, it is too sparingly used for its great potential as a bridge between individual student and teacher. However, it is generously used for those special students who make the teaching job a satisfying one. Teachers look at these students and say, with the expressions on their faces and the intensity of their glances, "I know you are learning, and I am proud of your work." And these students respond by visual contact, "I am learning. You are a good teacher." Other students in every classroom never receive these approving glances from teachers. They may go from class to class during the day without having meaningful, positive visual contact with any teacher.

No teacher decides to avoid exchanging glances with these students. It just happens that way because the teacher is not fully aware of the potential of nonverbal language. It can also be caused because the students have learned to avoid trying to make visual contact with their teachers. Their egos have been injured too many times.

If a teacher wants to check the validity of the direct eye contact message, he should pay particular attention to the number and kind of glances given to good students. Then, using that glance as a model, he might try it on a student who seldom excels in the teacher's estimation. The results will be surprising over the course of several weeks. If the teacher includes the student with verbal messages, reinforced by visual contacts that say, "I care," the student will begin to participate, to become involved, and to become free to learn.

Anyone who has been on the school premises for any length of time will soon learn to recognize the favorite gesture of many educators—the *pointed finger*. He will see teachers crooking a finger to beckon a student, pointing a straight index finger at the student's eyes, moving a finger elliptically to direct the student from one place to another, and wagging a finger to accuse a student of misconduct. What does it mean in the nonverbal language of education? Simply that the object of all this pointing and wagging is the student. Principals do not point at superintendents while they talk to them. Seldom do principals point at secretaries or custodians. Indeed, we do not point or gesture menacingly at any person whose status we consider to be equal to or greater than our own. It is easy to point at students because teachers and other adults in the school assume a dominant, superior attitude.

This attitude helps the teacher increase the distance from the student. In their arsenal, teachers and administrators have hundreds of cues of avoidance that can effectively maintain the distance. The stares, eye-rolls, thrown hands, shrugs, and the glances that overlook or see around and beyond the student all effectively inhibit student communication. The tragic mistake is that we act badly to youngsters and continue to do so again and again, even when we are trying to instruct them. The message is that we are unapproachable. We say to them, "If you want to catch our attention, to communicate with us, you must shock us into recognition of your existence, of your worth." And, when the student does shock teachers and principals, he may receive the attention and understanding that he needs, or we may increase the distance. Either way, teacher and student have missed the true communication that leads to the joy of learning, of working together.

If we want to conserve educational time, teach children, and not waste our energies in criticizing and correcting misbehavior, we should at least reexamine our verbal and nonverbal behavior.

How to Become a Better Communicator

How can we improve our awareness and use of nonverbal indicators to communicate more effectively? Whether working in a classroom or with one student, supervising fellow workers, or training a new employee, some basic behaviors have been categorized as encouraging to communication:

1. **Enthusiastic Support.** Enthusiastic support is demonstrated by unusual warmth for others. Nonverbal indicators are smiles and nods, warm greetings, a pat on the back, or any act that shows obvious approval. Vocal intonation or inflection can also indicate approval and support.

2. **Helping.** Spontaneous reactions to a request for help show that you are not reluctant to become involved. Your expression signifies acceptance of the problem as real, and your vocal in-

tonation reinforces this. You are interested in assisting, not putting the student on trial for the lack of knowledge or skill.

3. **Receptivity.** A willingness to listen with patience and interest to the other person is evident. Maintaining eye contact indicates patience and attention. Gestures and postures subtly encourage the individual to continue talking. You verbally encourage the person to continue talking by injecting comments such as "Yes," "Go on," "Okay," or "I'm listening" at appropriate points.

Some behaviors that have been shown to discourage communication are:

1. **Inattention.** Unwillingness or inability to be attentive. Avoiding eye contact. Gestures and postures that show impatience, preoccupation, or concern with other thoughts—thinking your own thoughts rather than listening.

2. **Unresponsive.** Failure to respond when a response would be expected, withdrawing from a request for help. Your gestures suggest tension or nervousness and you interrupt the person who is talking.

3. **Disapproval.** Frowning, scowling, threatening glances tend to inhibit others' efforts to communicate. Derisive, sarcastic, or disdainful expressions are used. Pointed fingers poke fun, belittle, or threaten the other person. Vocal tones are hostile, cross, irritated, or antagonistic. A shake of the head or a facial expression reveals a negative evaluation.

MEASURING NONVERBAL BEHAVIOR

When teachers and administrators realize that nonverbal communication is playing a significant part in the climate of their schools, they often ask if there are ways to measure educators' encouraging and inhibiting communicative behaviors.

A number of systems have been devised in recent years to record and examine teachers' verbal behaviors. Nonverbal behaviors are more difficult to analyze. We cannot see ourselves when we behave. If we lived in a "world of mirrors" perhaps we could manipulate our nonverbal language as easily as our verbal. Lacking that, there are three other methods of observing our nonverbal behavior: filming teacher episodes for later playback and analysis; using trained observers; and paying careful attention to the responses of students. As a practical matter, teachers who care about their nonverbal performance most often notice responses of students. However, teachers seem to differ markedly in their ability to sense the reactions of students.

To give teachers and others a model on which to build an observation system, we have used the Flanders Interaction Analysis system for a verbal and nonverbal approach. The Flanders system focuses primarily on the social-emotional climate of the classroom. Using its categories, we have developed relevant categories of nonverbal behavior.

The categories of the Flanders system are combined with nonverbal responses that have been identified as encouraging and restricting to communication. The resulting combination is:

Indirect-Direct (verbal)	Encouraging-Restricting (nonverbal)
Accepts student feeling	Acceptance-Indifference
Praises or encourages	Congruent-Incongruent
Uses student idea	Implement-Perfunctory
Asks questions	Personal-Impersonal
Lectures—gives information	Responsive-Unresponsive
Gives directions	Involve-Dismiss
Criticizes or justifies authority	Firm-Harsh
Student talk (responsive)	Receptive-Inattentive
Student talk (initiated)	Receptive-Inattentive
Silence of confusion	Comfort-Distress

This system is designed to allow the observer to use the categories, time intervals, and ground rules of the original Flanders system while also recording the nonverbal dimensions of teaching.

The Encouraging-Restricting Model

Another method of observing teacher nonverbal responses is to view nonverbal communication on a continuum from encouraging to restricting communication. Nonverbal communication that is **encouraging** has these ten characteristics:

1. Congruity between verbal intent and nonverbal behavior
2. Responsive to feedback from others
3. Positive affectivity or warmth and acceptance
4. Attentive to others, willing to listen
5. Responsive to student need
6. Supportive of pupil behavior
7. Intimate contact
8. Inclusive relationship
9. Unrestricted time
10. Open use of space

Nonverbal communication that is **restricting** has these characteristics:

1. Discrepancy between verbal intent and nonverbal behavior
2. Unresponsive to feedback from others
3. Negative affectivity or coldness or indifference
4. Inattentive to others
5. Unreceptive to student need

6. Disapproval of pupil behavior
7. Distant contact
8. Exclusive relationship
9. Restricted time
10. Closed space

Congruous—Incongruous—This dimension refers to the degree of congruity between the voice tone, gesture, and actions of the teacher and the verbal message. Congruity occurs when the teacher's verbal message is supported and reinforced by nonverbal behaviors. A mixed message or incongruity exists when there is a discrepancy or contradiction between the verbal message and the teacher's inflection and gesture. For example, a teacher who demands that assignments be turned in on time and does not grade or return them promptly displays incongruous behavior.

Responsiveness—Unresponsiveness—A responsive act is a modification in the teacher's behavior as a result of feedback. Verbal feedback occurs when the teacher hears himself talking, but nonverbal feedback is based on the reactions and responses of pupils to the teacher. A responsive act occurs when the teacher alters the pace or direction of a lesson after detecting misunderstanding or pupil distress. Unresponsive acts are ignoring the behavioral responses of pupils.

Positive—Negative Affectivity—Positive nonverbal expressions convey warm feelings, high regard, cheerful enthusiasm, and liking and acceptance. Negative nonverbal expressions convey aloofness, coldness, low regard, indifference, or rejection.

Attentive—Inattentive—Nonverbal expressions that imply a willingness to listen with patience and interest to pupil talk are attentive behaviors. By paying attention, the teacher shows interest in the pupil. By being inattentive or disinterested, the teacher inhibits the flow of communication from pupils and neither sustains nor encourages sharing information or expressing ideas.

Facilitating—Unreceptive—The teacher is facilitating when performing functions which help a pupil, usually in response to a detection of pupil needs or problems. An unreceptive act openly ignores a pupil when a response would ordinarily be expected. The teacher may ignore a question or request.

Supportive—Disapproving—Supportive expressions clearly show the teacher is pleased and approves of student behavior. Disapproving expressions convey dissatisfaction, discouragement, disparagement, or punishment. The facial expression may be one of frowning, scowling, or threatening glances.

Intimate—Distant—Teachers indicate how close and intimate their contacts with students are. Intimacy is revealed by physical proximity and psychological closeness, while distance is created by an absence of contact and a treatment of aloofness and withdrawal.

Inclusive—Exclusive—Nonverbal cues of action and glance reveal who is included or excluded. Inclusion is marked by exchanges or mutual glance and acknowledgment, while cues of exclusion suggest a denial that the other person is there or deserves recognition. Evidences of human existence or invisibility can be noted.

Free—Restricted Time—Definitions of our uses of time with others create realities beyond words. How much time we spend with others and how our time is used make a difference. Uses of time and the values we hold have a positive correlation.

Open—Closed Space—Classroom spaces outline travel routes of movement, and desks take on the property of territorial rights. Accessibility to the spaces and territories of the school becomes available or is inhibited.

There are real prospects that it will be possible to train teachers to be more knowledgeable about nonverbal communication in the classroom. Does this mean that teachers will be expected to qualify as psychologists, to discover meanings that lurk in the slightest movement of a child's head or a flicker of an eyelid? Not at all. Instead, the purpose will be to help teachers become aware of nonverbal cues, because they do exist in the classroom and do influence the business of teaching and learning.

To prove to yourself that nonverbal influences are operating now and can be directed to improve your work, try some of the following experiments. Then devise experiments of your own that you think might improve communication and participation in your classroom.

1. If you customarily work with small groups, experiment with the spread of the chairs. When the chairs are touching each other do the children react differently than when the chairs are a foot

apart? Does it make a difference whether you sit on a taller chair or on one the same height as the children's?

2. Use devices such as a bell to tell children you want their attention. Or flick the lights to show that a period is about to end. Nonverbal signals are often preferable to words, and many studies show that the teacher's voice is heard too often.

3. Make a conscious effort to teach to signals. A kindergarten teacher found that she would avoid calamities and classroom disruptions by observing more closely a boy with bathroom problems. The child chewing his pencil may be hoping you will come to his desk.

4. Try to match your nonverbal behavior to the child's and examine the results. For instance, sometimes teachers tend to be overarticulate with a nonarticulate child, subconsciously compensating for his lacks. A child who sits quietly beside the teacher may be getting warmth and support as the teacher sits quietly too. Matching the nonverbal behavior of a child is a kind of approval.

5. Experiment with light and heat in the classroom. Deliberate changes in temperature can be an effective device for changing classroom atmosphere. Artificial light is often unnecessary on a sunny day.

6. Use pictures rather than words in classroom displays and signs. One teacher experimented with two signs. The first said: "Pick up paper and put it in the wastebasket." The second was a silhouette of a child dropping paper in the wastebasket. The second proved to be more effective.

7. Talk about nonverbal communication, particularly with older children. Give them the opportunity to express their opinions and feelings about adults' nonverbal behavior.

8. Increase your practice of looking a student in the eye. Let the student look at you when he talks without exchanging a dominant gaze.

9. Increase the frequency of your relevant gestures. Let the movement of hands and arms punctuate and support your verbal explanations.

10. Experiment with new movement patterns. Do routine things differently. You may be making yourself too available or not available enough.

11. Let the students experiment with furniture arrangements

that involve group interaction. One teacher tried putting desks in groups with children facing each other. Two days later the desks were reversed so that the children faced away from each other.

12. Individualize your attention. You can't listen to all of the children all of the time, so experiment with listening very intently to a child for a brief period. As long as he is talking, look directly at him.

CONCLUSION

How has nonverbal communication come to assume such importance in our everyday life? With an absence of information, human beings fear the worst. They assign to the behaviors of others the meanings that characterize their worst fears. Failing to know how one stands and what perceptions are held by others, a person projects anxious uncertainty, which extends to the expressive behaviors of others. Nonverbal sources of communication assume preeminence when verbal information is lacking or missing. Part of the press to emphasize the power of nonverbal influence is to recognize the need for clarity and accuracy in verbal communication. When words fail to convey meaning or when verbal contacts are minimal, a heavy load must be carried by nonverbal channels. The urgency to be understood well and to understand others is to recognize the need to communicate full information. When verbal statements of thought and feeling are withheld from communicative contacts, then leakages and extra signs of nonverbal information fill the void.

When a person cannot succeed in making accurate predictions of interpersonal regard from communicative contacts, he becomes uncertain. Anxiety sets in, deterring future interactions. All of us need to send complete messages that combine to create congruency. When a discrepancy or inconsistency exists between what is said and what is expressed, we become confused. We would like to believe the verbal but suffer difficulty when the nonverbal reveals something else. We do know that a person is more likely to place greater faith and reliance on the nonverbal when a choice must be made.

To become more knowledgeable and sensitive to the influences of nonverbal communication is a demanding task. The best way to start is to develop an awareness of the multiplicity of messages. Human beings send and receive information multisensorily. If we see and hear more sensitively, then a richer and more available source of data exists for creating understanding. But awareness does not come all at once. Accuracy improves as perception increases. When we perceive to greater depths, we are more attuned to those around us and we begin to employ nonverbal cues for positive purposes. We begin to recognize that expressive cues transmit emotions and feelings more quickly than speech. Verbal contacts can initiate meaningful exchanges of thought and feeling, but nonverbal messages confirm the credibility and fidelity of intent. When we learn to become more aware of the fragility and difficulty of communicating well, then we begin to recognize the profound contribution of the silent, yet thunderous impact of nonverbal language.